by Judith Herbst

Lerner Publications Company • Minneapolis

Lerner Publications Company
A division of Lerner Publishing Group
241 First Avenue North
Minneapolis, Minnesota 55401 U.S.A.

Website address: www.lernerbooks.com

Library of Congress Cataloging-in-Publication Data

Herbst, Judith.
　　ESP / by Judith Herbst.
　　　　p.　cm. — (The unexplained)
　　Includes index.
　　Contents: Nostradamus jam — Mind over matter — Yes, but how do you know you know? — Seeing is deceiving.
　　ISBN: 0–8225–1628–4 (lib. bdg. : alk. paper)
　　1. Extrasensory perception [1. Extrasensory perception.]　I. Title: Extrasensory perception.　II. Series: Unexplained (Lerner Publications)
　　BF1321.H39　2005
　　133.8—dc22　　　　　　　　　　　　　　　　　　2003026462

Manufactured in the United States of America
1 2 3 4 5 6 – JR – 10 09 08 07 06 05

Table of Contents

Between the idea

And the reality

Between the motion

And the act

Falls the Shadow.

— T. S. Eliot

CHAPTER 1

NOSTRADAMUS JAM

A glittering Ferris wheel turns lazily against the starry night. Thick waves of fried dough roll through the air and collide with an advancing cotton candy front. Balloons bob like buoys. In the center of it all, a wooden roller coaster roars on a steel track that will be gone in a week. Just beyond the lights, along the half-darkened midway, slippery carny men reel in their prey with promises of stuffed bears and hula girl lamps. "Ring the bottles!" they shout. "Win a prize!" Everywhere there is magic. Time hangs like a held breath. You look around hastily and slip into the tent.

The Gypsy woman is framed in orange light. Her blue-lidded eyes are closed. Her long fingers are spread like spiders on the table in front of her. There is a crystal ball and a fan of tarot cards. She has been waiting for you all her life. Slowly, she opens her eyes and invites you to sit down. She will tell you what the future holds.

Fortune-telling is as old as time. Whether we are impatient or just curious, we have always wanted to know what fate has in store for us. And there has never been a shortage of seers willing to accommodate us, as long as we cross their palms with silver.

When it comes to prophets, no one has ever had more followers than

Nostradamus. He has been credited with predicting the death of France's King Henry II, the invention of the hot-air balloon, the rise and fall of Adolf Hitler, both World Wars, and a colorful assortment of catastrophes and earth-shattering events, including the end of the world. The list is impressive.

Born Michel de Notredame in Provence, France, in 1503, Nostradamus studied

Nostradamus has been famous for his predictions for centuries.

to be a doctor. He received his medical degree in 1529 and set up practice four years later, just in time for the plague. In those days, there wasn't much Nostradamus could do for his patients, but he tried his best and quickly came to be known as the plague doctor. With all this celebrity, you'd think he'd want to write his memoirs, but he decided instead to publish a cook-book. Nostradamus made a very tasty strawberry jam.

THE PROPHET IS A PSYCHIC

ESP stands for extrasensory perception. It is said to be a way of receiving information through supernatural means. A psychic is someone who claims to use supernatural means to move objects, heal people's illnesses, communicate with the dead, and gain information. A prophet is a psychic who claims the ability to gain knowledge about the future.

Sales were brisk, but Nostradamus had a hunch he could do even better if he wrote an almanac. Sixteenth-century almanacs were spicy, indeed, featuring plenty of astrological predictions—not that Nostradamus thought of himself as a prophet. But he had studied astrology in medical school and could cast a horoscope with the best of them. So Nostradamus published his first almanac in 1550. The following year, he came out with another one and before long had earned the reputation of someone who could foretell the future.

Pleased by this unexpected success, Nostradamus decided to capitalize on the public's fascination with soothsaying and sorcery. (At the time, there were about 30,000 psychics, magicians, and mystics in the city of Paris alone!) So he sat down and composed a batch of four-line poetic verses called quatrains. In 1555 he published them. Eventually, they became known by the title *Centuries,* because they totaled 100.

The horoscope is a very old device for predicting the future. It relies on the positions and the rising and setting times and dates of the sun, moon, and planets. While these bodies have slight gravitational effects on each other, predicting the future based on those relationships has no scientific foundation whatsoever.

Centuries was billed as a book of prophetic visions, and within four months of its appearance, a very impressed Catherine de Médicis, the superstitious queen of France, invited Nostradamus to visit the palace. Everyone in power was deeply interested in what the future held. Will I succeed to the throne? Will I enjoy a long reign? Be assassinated? Conquered by invaders? Exiled? Betrayed by enemies? There was a lot to worry about, and *Centuries,* with its wealth of information, seemed to be a kind of early-warning system. Deeply grateful, the rulers of France welcomed Nostradamus with open arms as well as open purses, proclaiming him the Seer of Provence.

But *Centuries* could hardly be called straightforward, let's-get-right-to-the-point stuff. Nostradamus's poetry proved to be murky, vague, and open to a lot of different interpretations. Here's an example:

From a simple soldier he will attain to empire,
From a short robe he will attain to the long.
Valiant in arms, in the church he is the worst,
Vexing the priests like water does the sponge.

This seems like a prediction, but what, exactly, is Nostradamus predicting? Well, that's obvious in the first line, you may think. A simple soldier is going to rule an empire. Fine, but whom is Nostradamus talking about? Many people believe the verse refers to the French emperor Napoleon. But the wording gives no clue whatsoever. The "soldier" could just as easily be Dwight D. Eisenhower, who, after serving in the military, became president of the United States. Fidel Castro of Cuba would also fill the bill, as would half a dozen other leaders. So how valuable is this verse as a prediction?

Another reason to question Nostradamus's "gift" is the terrible problem nearly everyone had with his handwriting. It was downright awful!

"I have finally received," wrote Lorenz Tubbe, one of Nostradamus's astrology clients, "with great pleasure, your letter and the horoscope. Alas! Your handwriting and the text gave me problems. Since I don't know French, I had to appeal to French friends, but it's impossible to decipher you!"

Nostradamus, of course, couldn't use a typewriter, as it hadn't been invented yet. He had to write everything—including his *Centuries* manuscript—in longhand. If Tubbe's French friends had trouble deciphering Nostradamus, there's a good chance that the people who translated *Centuries* from French also had trouble. And we can't even refer to the original manuscript, because it no longer exists. So the verses that people interpret as true

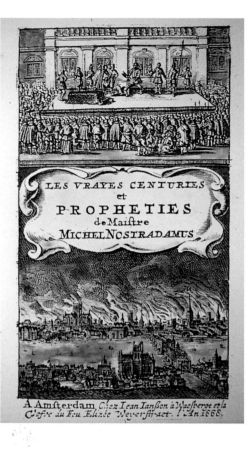

The title page of the 1668 edition of *Centuries* depicts two of Nostradamus's predictions: the execution of England's King Charles I (1649) and the Great Fire of London (1666).

prophecies may not even say what Nostradamus intended.

Misunderstandings and mistranslations abound. One of Nostradamus's most famous quatrains contains the name Hister. Most of Nostradamus's followers think this really means Hitler. But Hister is actually an old name for the Danube, a river in Germany. Once you know that, Nostradamus's Hitler predictions fall to pieces.

And then we have the predictions that are just flat-out wrong. Here is an example:

> The year that Saturn and Mars are conjunct and combust
> The air will be very dry and there will be a long trajection,
> Through incendiarism a great locality will be consumed by fire,
> There will be little rain, with wind, heat, wars and incursions.

Lee McCann, author of the 1941 book *Nostradamus: The Man Who Saw through Time,* somehow saw this quatrain as the prediction of an April

Nostradamus (*above*) at work in his office. His vague predictions have been open to interpretation by many believers.

1998 total solar eclipse and a massive invasion of France. The invasion didn't occur, and the eclipse was on March 9.

But Nostradamus is so famous, you may be thinking. Surely he got *something* right. Actually, he did, but he wasn't really seeing into the future. There is no question that Nostradamus was clever, talented, and well educated. He also did a lot of traveling. He rubbed elbows with kings and understood the political climate. All this helped him to make pretty good guesses about the kinds of things that might happen. Modern political analysts do this all the time.

>> Future Tense

One of the most popular modern-day American psychics was Jeane Dixon. (She died in 1997.) Dixon burst onto the psychic scene in March 1956 when she predicted in *Parade* magazine that a Democratic president elected in 1960 would die in office.

American psychic Jeane Dixon is most famous for her prediction of President John F. Kennedy's assassination.

When John F. Kennedy was indeed killed by an assassin's bullet in 1963, Dixon was hailed as a true prophet. But was she really?

Predicting the death of a president is very risky. At the time of Dixon's proclamation, 7 presidents out of a total of 35 had died while in office. So what was the probability that Kennedy would not live to serve out his term? Statistically, it was one in five—a 20 percent chance. Still, Dixon declared he would die, if not during his first term, then in the second. She had to have foreseen it, right?

Well, maybe not. It's possible that Dixon was simply relying on the so-called presidential curse. This is not a curse, as such. It's just one of those quirky patterns that people love to use to predict what will happen next. It seems that each of the U.S. presidents elected every 20 years, starting with William Henry Harrison in 1840, has died while in office. (By surviving an attempt on his life, Ronald Reagan, who was elected in 1980, seems to have "broken" the so-called curse.) Of course, the deaths were just a coincidence, and not even a very valid one because Zachary Taylor didn't follow the pattern. Elected in 1848, Taylor served 16 months and died in 1850. But because the "curse" won't work if you include Taylor's death, it's generally ignored.

In any event, Franklin Roosevelt died in 1945, during his fourth term. So Kennedy would have been the next to die, according to the "curse." And Dixon was careful to say that his death would "not necessarily occur in his first term," which increased the odds that her prediction would come true. But if Jeane Dixon based her prediction on this bogus presidential curse, she showed a lot of guts. What if she had been wrong?

Here's the answer. Everyone would have said, "Thank heaven she was wrong! President Kennedy is alive!" In other words, it wouldn't have mattered because her prediction was so dire. But sadly, she was right, so does this mean she foresaw the future? You decide, but before you do, consider the following Jeane Dixon predictions:

- Russia will be the first country to put a man on the Moon.
- The year 1958 will see the start of World War III.
- A woman will become the U.S. president in the 1980s.
- A huge comet will strike the earth before the end of the twentieth century.
- In 1999 the United States and its allies will enter a war with Russia, and Russian missiles "will rain down in a nuclear holocaust."

Big predictions, all wrong. But does anybody remember them? No, because once a psychic has established a reputation, people tend to ignore the failures.

To be fair, however, Jeane Dixon did, occasionally, come through. But like Nostradamus before her and those who have followed her, many of her successes can be attributed to educated guesses.

There are ways to make predictions without special powers. One technique some psychics use is generalization. They make vague statements and don't give any dates. Joseph DeLouise, a hairdresser turned psychic, predicted that human beings would win the war against air pollution. He did not say when. Richard McClintic said that a new cure for blood diseases would be discovered sometime in the future. That certainly leaves the door open.

On the other hand, psychics who confidently declare when things will happen are using a psychological technique. They are saying, "Trust me! I'm sure!" Of course, they may not be sure at all. They may even be guessing, but the public doesn't know that. What the public hears is someone who has no doubt whatsoever that he or she is a prophet, and this leads to something called circular reasoning.

In other words, because this person is billing himself or herself as a prophet, people are ready to believe it.

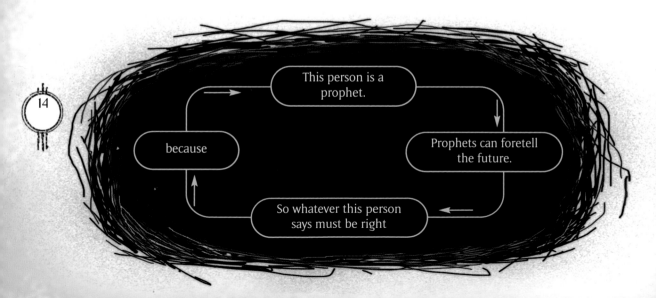

This person is a prophet.

Prophets can foretell the future.

So whatever this person says must be right

because

>> Hits and Misses

How do you tell the real prophets from the frauds, fakers, and show-business performers? Are there any real prophets? As a general rule of thumb, someone who has a psychic ability to predict the future should be able to do it more often and more accurately than chance would allow. But you have seen that there are ways to increase the success rate. So perhaps our standards should be higher. If someone is truly a prophet, should he or she be dishing out nonsense like this?

- On June 9, 1989, Denver will be wiped out by "pressure" from outer space ("The Amazing" Criswell).
- Sometime between 1975 and 1980, the water level in New York will rise and flood the city out of existence (Malcolm Bessent).
- A "Thought-Action-Deed Machine" will be invented in 1986, and scientists will be able to tune into events from the past, present, and future (David Bubar).
- Between November and December 1980, Pennsylvanians will suffer an outbreak of cannibalism caused by an experiment that goes haywire (Criswell again).

If these so-called psychics did make a few predictions that seemed to have come true, should they be excused for dishing out this claptrap? Maybe we should say, "Either you can see into the future, or you can't!"

But it might not be that simple. Haven't we all had a premonition, a vague feeling that something was going to happen? Usually, we can't say what it is exactly. We just have a kind of prickly sense. Other times, the feeling is more specific. "Oh gosh," you may say, "I just know we're going to have a quiz tomorrow!" Could our premonitions be the outer edge of ESP?

Most scientists would say no. Generally, when we anticipate something happening, it's because we have tuned into subtle, but very concrete, clues. Your teacher, for example, likes to give pop quizzes and hasn't done so in a while. So with each day that passes, the chances of a surprise quiz go up. Nothing psychic here.

And yet . . . there are those predictions that seem so much like genuine prophecy, you have to wonder if the person tapped into some unknown force. But what could it be, and how could someone tap into it?

As you might expect, traditional science does not like precognition for a couple of reasons. First, precognition—which means "knowing in advance"—suggests that information about the future is reaching the psychic through some sort of sixth sense. It's a reasonable assumption because it is through our senses that we gain knowledge about our world. But what could this sixth sensory organ possibly be? Why isn't it as obvious as our eyes and ears? How does information about the future reach the psychic?

How, indeed? Like everything else that exists in nature, this information has to be made of something. That "something" is subatomic particles—tiny, tiny packets of energy.

There are many different kinds of subatomic particles, and they move at different speeds. But the fastest are the photons, particles of light, which travel at roughly 186,000 miles a second. The speed of light is a magic number because only photons can travel this fast, and nothing can travel any faster. Here's why.

Albert Einstein discovered that as an object approaches light speed, time begins to slow down. At light speed *exactly,* time stands still. But if

PRECOGNITION?

David Bubar predicted that a major hurricane would hit the East Coast in the summer of 1969. He was right, but summer is smack in the middle of hurricane season, and the East Coast is often a target. Precognition or just a logical guess? In 1968 Joseph DeLouise predicted space disasters for the United States and Russia. He was also right, but because space travel is so incredibly dangerous, this was a prediction that almost anybody could have made. Shawn Robbins predicted that a country beginning with the letter "I" would suffer "terrible earth disasters." Iran, Iraq, India, Indonesia, and Iceland are all prone to earthquakes. So Robbins waited, and sure enough, her prediction came true.

you could somehow travel faster than light, time would start to go backward. Since a person with precognition supposedly receives information about the future, the information has to travel *into the past* to reach that person. That means it has to move faster than light. What particles carry the information? Not photons. They can move only *at* light speed. Some scientists think there may be faster-than-light particles. But even though they have named them tachyons (from a Greek word meaning "speed"), nobody has ever found one. So how does the "prophet" get the information?

You are no doubt waiting for the final answer to the question, "Can some people predict the future?" But you read the chapter. What do you think?

CHAPTER 2
MIND OVER MATTER

She sits alone in a room with four pairs of eyes watching behind a one-way glass. Her iron-gray hair springs away from her head, suggestive of a steel wool pad. Her face, lined with 60 years of life, is twisted into a knot of concentration. The experimenters have scattered paper clips on the table in front of her. It has come to their attention that this woman with the Russian name can move things with her mind. She can make dice fall to snake eyes. She can urge spinning quarters to land eagle up—or down. You call it. She has a talent of questionable worth, but they are studying it anyway.

The woman's hands hover above the paper clips like UFOs. The experimenters watch from the next room. "They're moving," one of them whispers. "She's doing it." The woman has broken out into a sweat. It's a great show.

Psychokinesis, or PK, from two Greek words meaning "mind movement," is the ability to affect objects without the use of physical means. Right off the bat, this sounds impossible. But when the Great Rinaldo invites his lovely chiffon-clad assistant to lie down on a table and then proceeds to levitate her, it sure looks like PK. Rinaldo slips a

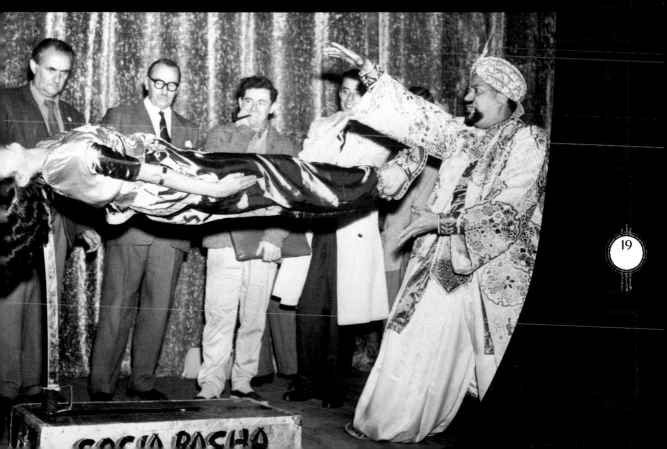

Magician Gogia Pasha appears to levitate his hypnotized daughter, Usha, on the point of a sword.

The Indian Rope Trick

For centuries the Indian rope trick has been shrouded in mystery—not to mention incense. A gawking audience sees the fakir toss a heavy rope up in the air, where it remains, swaying tantalizingly in the soft breeze. Then the fakir or a young assistant scrambles up the rope and disappears into a heavy cloud of incense. But it is what you don't see within all that incense that turns the seemingly supernatural into a good old-fashioned magic trick.

The fakir prepares the scene by running a thin but strong wire between two trees. Billowing clouds of incense rise to obscure the wire. The stage is set. At the performance, the fakir tosses the rope—at the end of which is a hook—high into the air. The hook catches the wire, and the rope appears to hang in midair. If you don't know how the trick works, it's a great show.

hula hoop over his floating assistant to prove there are no strings attached. He walks all around her. "See?" he seems to be saying. "It's not done with mirrors either." But seeing should not lead to believing, and even though the levitation looks real, it's just an illusion.

People who claim genuine PK ability basically do what the Great Rinaldo does—although rarely in such a spectacular way. They say they can influence the toss of a coin, move furniture, and get scattered paper clips to cluster together all by mind power alone. But how do we know that they, too, are not clever magicians? Until PK is a proven ability, one must always look for the trick.

>> Catch Me if You Can

In the 1800s, the salons and drawing rooms of the United States were all abuzz with talk of Daniel Dunglas Home. Home (pronounced *Hume*) was simply fabulous, people said, a spirit medium who could call up your dead grandpappy, bam! Just like that! He could convince spirits to appear and then hover for a time above the heads of the assembled believers.

He could move tables and chairs across a room with the wink of an eye, play instruments without touching them, and actually levitate himself. At the time, nobody put on a more convincing show, and Home didn't even charge for his séances. (This did not, however, prevent him from accepting lavish gifts from his wealthy fan club.) He was popular and successful, and he was also one of the first psychics to be investigated.

A drawing of Home supposedly levitating himself

Sir William Crookes

The scientist who looked into Home's act was the British physicist Sir William Crookes. Crookes had turned to spiritualism after the unexpected death of his beloved brother. He, like so many others, may have been desperate for the comfort that mediums can sometimes provide. If you believe that a medium can actually contact the dead, then your connection with a loved one will not be broken. The medium seems to offer proof that instead of being "gone," the deceased is merely "somewhere else." Emotionally, it's very attractive. So Crookes threw himself into spiritualism and in 1883 joined the newly established Society for Psychical Research. It was during this time that he met and became friends with Daniel Home.

Under the society's banner, Crookes investigated a number of spirit mediums. Some he showed to be frauds. Others (who were also frauds) were able to fool him, probably because Crookes was a physical scientist, not an expert in trickery and sleight of hand. When it comes to psychic fraud detection, it usually takes one to know one.

Crookes sat in on Home's séances more than a few times, checking for any signs of funny business as Home made ghostly hands appear and levitated the furniture. Crookes was duly impressed with Home's psychic abilities and declared his friend absolutely genuine. Others also tried to find the tricks up Home's sleeves, but no one was successful, and Home died with his reputation as solid as a rock.

But it must be noted that Home was always very careful to control the conditions of his séances. He never made house calls, preferring instead to conduct the sessions in his own drawing room. The participants were handpicked, and cameras were never allowed. On the other hand, Home insisted that the lights be left on and even invited everyone to watch him closely for signs of trickery. But stage magicians also perform with the lights on, and no matter how closely you watch, you still don't see anything.

Home may have actually left behind a clue that he was not entirely on the up-and-up. He had an act in which he made an accordion play without touching it. The accordion was locked in a wire cage, but it had to be placed under the table at which he sat, with the keys against the floor. This setup was very important. With the accordion in this position, nobody could see if the keys were actually moving. Home then slipped his hand through the bars of the cage and extended the bellows.

Levitation and a ghostly hand? Probably not. In a séance, heavy drapes, secret doors, and darkness can hide a lot of not-so-otherworldly props and assistants.

UPSY-DAISY!

One of the oldest tricks in the psychic handbook is levitation. Through mind power alone, we are told, a psychic can cause a volunteer to rise into the air like a balloon. But this is all just a terrific example of the power of physics. Four assistants (or sometimes three plus the psychic) place their index fingers under the knees and armpits of the volunteer and lift. Even though the lifters are using only two fingers, the volunteer's weight has been evenly distributed, making it a cinch to perform the "levitation."

Extending the bellows is what a magician would call a diversion, because it was the hand holding open the bellows that everybody watched. If Home were going to cheat, this was the hand he would have to use to play the accordion. (His other hand was on the table.)

Home, however, did not play the accordion. He didn't have to. There was another way he could have produced the sound, and it had nothing to do with PK.

After Home died, several tiny harmonicas were found among his belongings. Had he hidden one in his mouth and played *that* instead of relying on PK to move the accordion's keys? It's certainly possible. It would have taken a bit of practice, but Home could have done it. In fact, others have. And everyone who was present for Home's accordion routine agreed that the music was always very thin and faint. It sort of makes you wonder if Crookes's investigations had been sufficiently thorough.

>> Geller's Gifts?

In the 1970s and 1980s, self-proclaimed psychic Uri Geller was nothing short of a phenomenon. In addition to being handsome and charming, he did something no one else had ever done. He made silverware bend and then break by . . . the power of his mind? Could that be true?

Geller started out as a fashion model and small-time magician before he was discovered, repackaged, and presented on British television in 1973 as a young man with a gift. To the amazement of just about everyone, Geller read messages in sealed envelopes and demonstrated what looked like genuine PK by restarting broken watches, making compass needles turn, and decapitating spoons. Audiences loved him. When skeptics pointed out that magicians and conjurers could do the same thing, Geller waved them off. He never used tricks, he said. He didn't have to. He had the gift.

Before long, parapsychologists Russell Targ and Harold Puthoff invited Geller to join them in the research lab. After running Geller through a series of guess-the-picture tests, dice tests, and the like, Targ and Puthoff published their results. Their paper, which appeared in the scientific journal *Nature,* declared Geller a genuine psychic. But when Ray Hyman looked into the conditions under which Geller had been tested, he discovered that the procedures had been "sloppy and inadequate." Targ and Puthoff denied the charge,

Uri Geller performs his famous spoon-bending trick.

and there the matter rested, but not very comfortably.

In 1974 Henry Puharich, an M.D. with some very wacko interests, somehow got it into his head that Geller's powers had been a gift from the beings on a planet called Hoova. Amazingly, this jewel of all stupid suggestions boosted Geller's popularity several notches. People flocked to see Geller's act, and Geller became a favorite with just about everybody except the magicians' union.

In 1985 the Australian conjurer Ben Harris published a book explaining how to bend spoons and other metallic objects. Magicians in Norway and Sweden followed with books that showed how to do Geller's watch trick, in which Geller made the hands move without help from the watch stem.

So Geller has been unmasked, but he has refused to give up. In the late 1980s, he offered his services to the National Aeronautics and Space Administration (NASA). He would be glad, he said, to use PK to "float" home a camera left on the Moon's surface by the Apollo astronauts. The camera, as far as anybody knows, is still up there. Maybe NASA didn't want to pay Geller for the shipping.

>> All the Right Moves

Back in the 1970s, John Hasted, a physics professor at Birkbeck College in London, conducted several PK tests with young children. He put a generous helping of paper clips into a glass globe, left the kids alone for a while, and presto! When he returned, the paper clips were bent and twisted into a wiry mass. Well, if anything looked like real PK, this was certainly it. The test subjects were not flashy publicity seekers, but innocent children. Surely their hearts were pure.

Oh, really? Rule number one for parapsychologists who want to be taken seriously: never leave the subject alone with the test. Even kids can figure out ways to break seals, open locks, unhinge cabinets, and tamper with what a trusting tester believes is foolproof. Of course, in this case, the kids didn't have much to tamper with. There was a hole in the top of the globe. Who could resist? One can only imagine how much giggling went on when the kids found themselves all alone and left to their own devices. The truth came out when the tests were videotaped.

But testing for PK is getting tougher. Researchers no longer ask a subject to make jelly beans hop across a table. They have learned that

These children are being tested for their psychic abilities. They wear
"thinking caps" provided by the researcher to enhance their "powers"
and to make the exercise fun.

there are just too many ways to cheat. So the latest PK experiments pit
humans against machines. Machines are pretty much tamperproof, provided, of course, that the subject is not given a screwdriver and allowed to
take the machine home.

One of the machines used in PK tests is called the random event gener-
ator. It was developed by physicist Helmut Schmidt. Schmidt's machine
uses a radioactive substance, a Geiger counter, and a high-speed oscilla-
tor to generate numbers. The numbers translate into pulses that light up
one of eight bulbs on a clock face. But if the machine is complicated, the
test itself isn't. The subject simply sits down and tries to will the machine
to generate pulses that will light up the bulbs in a clockwise direction.
Ordinarily, the bulbs would light up randomly in either a clockwise or a
counterclockwise direction.

So, what's the score? Did Schmidt have any success with his test subjects?
Well, actually, a curious thing happened. Schmidt ran 32,786 trials. If pure

chance were operating, the pulse should randomly jump from one of the eight bulbs to the next in a clockwise direction 50 percent of the time. (The other 50 percent of the time, the pulse should jump counterclockwise.) But when Schmidt's subjects tried to influence the machine in a clockwise direction, the pulses jumped clockwise only 49 percent of the time. In other words, there was a negative effect!

What does this mean? Well, it might not mean anything because the negative effect is so small. Did Schmidt's subjects demonstrate PK? What do you think?

We close this chapter with what is certainly one of the wackiest PK experiments of all time. Two subjects, a "psychic" and a skeptic, faced off in front of a plant. The "psychic" worked on willing the plant to die. The skeptic concentrated on keeping the plant alive. The challengers stared intently at the plant for several minutes. When the plant remained alive and unchanged, the "psychic" blamed his failure on the skeptic's "negative energy." Wanna buy a bridge? We'll levitate it right to your door.

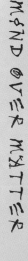

This is one of the first random event generators developed by Helmut Schmidt.

YES, BUT HOW DO YOU KNOW YOU KNOW?

"I am sensing," says the psychic who calls herself Mrs. Jones, "a soft fabric. Silk, perhaps, or satin. Maybe wool."

Her client nods. "Yes," she breathes, remembering the feel of her favorite blanket. "Wool."

The psychic smiles inwardly, relieved and encouraged, and continues to fish. "And there is a doll with a fancy dress."

This time, the woman frowns.

". . . Or perhaps not," oozes Mrs. Jones, smoothly backpedaling. "Another

kind of toy. Very cherished."

It is a good guess. "Yes," says the woman. "My Oakie."

Oakie? What's an Oakie? Could be anything, but sounds like a stuffed animal. A cat, maybe. This woman's wearing a ceramic cat pin. Go for it. "I see a toy cat."

"Yes!" cries the woman. "Yes! That's exactly right!"

Bingo! This'll be a cinch.

The first person to carry out formal studies on ESP was John Coover, who used an ordinary deck of playing cards to test over 100 subjects at Stanford University in 1917. G. H. Estabrooks followed Coover, and his early results were tantalizing. Rather than pulling from the general student population, Estabrooks chose subjects who were "positively interested." And lo and behold! They seemed to be very good at guessing the suit of the target card when in the same room as Estabrooks. But when Estabrooks moved them into a separate room, their scores dropped to mere chance. Why were the scores high only when the subject and the tester were in the same room? Could the subjects have been picking up on cues from the tester? Could they, in fact, have been cheating?

Joseph Banks Rhine came on the scene in 1928. He had a degree in botany and slid into parapsychology through the back door. Some years before, he had attended a lecture on spirits, mediums, and the like and decided this was for him. ESP research became his life.

Rhine's first test subject—believe it or not—was a horse. Lady Wonder of Richmond, Virginia, was supposedly able to

Lady Wonder uses her "typewriter" to answer questions. The one with the knowledge, though, was Lady Wonder's trainer, who had taught the horse to respond to his body movements and other cues.

make predictions and read people's minds, so Rhine went off to catch her act. He watched the demonstration, and because he couldn't come up with another explanation for the horse's amazing skills, he declared Lady Wonder a true psychic. It wasn't a very promising start for an ESP investigator who wanted to be taken seriously. Lady Wonder, of course, was not nearly as gifted as she was said to be. Some time later, the magician Milbourne Christopher showed how the tricks were done.

Rhine had found his calling, though, and he soon began conducting ESP tests on humans. In his tests for clairvoyance, Rhine asked adult subjects to identify the symbol on cards placed one at a time, facedown in front of them. To test for telepathy, a researcher tried to "send" the symbol on the card to the subject. Correct responses were called "hits." Incorrect responses were "misses." Rhine also ran tests on children, asking them to identify numbers.

The results of Rhine's early tests were disappointing. The scores were the same as they would have been if the subjects had been guessing. In other words, when the subjects were asked to guess a card's suit, they were correct one out of four times. This is what chance would predict. But Rhine was not discouraged, and in 1930, he teamed up with Karl Zener, who had developed a unique set of cards to test for ESP.

Rhine and Zener ran a whopping 1,600 trials, but none of the subjects showed even a hint of ESP ability. It was at this point that Zener threw in his hand, leaving behind the cards that bear his name. Rhine continued the tests and, curiously enough, started to get positive results. He gushed

Zener cards, developed by Karl Zener, are a set of five cards showing a star, a circle, a cross, wavy lines, and a square. These cards are used in testing psychic abilities.

Joseph Banks Rhine tests subjects using Zener cards.

that he had some very impressive evidence for ESP. Clairvoyance and telepathy, he declared, were entirely real. Well, with the careful Zener safely absent, Rhine's claims were a little suspicious. So a number of other researchers began running their own tests in an effort to duplicate Rhine's results. Not a single one succeeded. W. E. Cox ran 25,064 trials with 132 subjects at Princeton University but found "no evidence," as he put it, "of extrasensory perception." Rhine's results, he concluded, must have been due to "uncontrollable factors in the experimental procedure."

>> Perhaps a Hint of ESP?

Let us jump to the 1960s, when a mild-mannered bank clerk from Czechoslovakia named Pavel Stepanek intrigued the ESP researchers with his card-guessing feats. The cards used in the experiment were white on one side and black on the other. They were fitted with heavy cardboard covers and held up, one at a time, by a researcher. Stepanek tried to guess which color was face up. He had a 50-50 chance of being right each time. He could say the card was either white or black. So in 2,000 trials, pure guessing would produce 1,000 hits. Stepanek, however, guessed right 1,140 times, which gave him a score of 57 percent. But does that mean anything? Well, it's certainly better than chance, so the researchers figured they might have had something. The testing continued.

Over the next several years, a very patient Stepanek guessed, and guessed, and guessed. He continued to score a few percentage points above chance. Along the way, the experimenters began to wonder if Stepanek might be reading heat cues through the card covers. Since black surfaces absorb light, and white surfaces reflect it, a black surface will be warmer than a white surface. Most of us can't even feel such subtle temperature

differences, let alone see them, but perhaps Stepanek could. So the experimenters put the jacketed cards into another envelope, and then another, and another. And after a while, a very curious thing happened. Stepanek's ability to guess the cards' colors started to fade.

It's true that all this testing had gone on for more than 10 years. If Stepanek really had been clairvoyant, he might have just worn himself out. His ESP could have disappeared on its own, or it might not have been there in the first place. Stepanek could have been cheating. How? Who knows? But it is certainly coincidental that once the cards were thoroughly "insulated," Stepanek's scores dropped to mere chance. The researchers explained it by saying that Stepanek's ESP became "confused" by all those envelopes. Like a traveler faced with too many road signs, he didn't know which way to turn. Nevertheless, he had produced some remarkable scores, they said, and his talent deserved to be recognized.

If Stepanek, with his scores of 57 percent, was genuine, then ESP is subtle indeed. Stepanek, whom the *Guinness Book of World Records* book once called "the most psychic man," did not display, shall we say, 20/20 vision. He was wrong almost as often as he was right. But he guessed right enough times to nudge him up and over the bar we call probability, or chance. So maybe something was there, but just barely.

Some researchers have suggested that ESP is so fragile, it can be affected by "bad vibes" or "negative energy." Skeptics who attend testing sessions supposedly have so much negative energy that they can temporarily block the subject's ESP. They are parapsychology's version of the lead shield that blocks radiation. But this sounds suspiciously like an excuse. Every time a professional magician is in the room, the psychic loses his or her powers? That's rather convenient, don't you think? If the researchers want to claim "negative energy," they first have to prove it actually exists. Otherwise it's about as scientifically valid as pixie dust.

ESP is also said to be very unpredictable. Like the .400 batter who sometimes swings through pitch after pitch, clairvoyants can have good days and bad days. This may well be. But it certainly makes ESP harder to measure.

ESP could, of course, be in the process of evolving. Since the first cells appeared on our planet, living things have continually changed and developed. So perhaps we are slowly giving birth to a new kind of sense, one that will serve a future need. In some far-flung tomorrow, we may all be reading each other's minds.

Uh-oh.

CHAPTER 4
SEEING IS DECEIVING

"You're looking for a missile silo," said the colonel.

The man they called Quentin nodded. "Right."

"It probably looks something like this." The colonel pushed a black-and-white photograph across the desk. "We can't fly over where we think it is. Restricted airspace. Our drone would be shot down, and we don't want that."

Again, Quentin nodded. He knew the deal. He'd done this before.

"We need confirmation, is all," said the colonel. "And whatever else you see down there." He shifted his cigar. It had gone out long ago. "Ready to go?"

Quentin gave the colonel a thumbs-up sign and closed his eyes. His mind would do the rest.

Ingo Swann is a New York artist who claims to have traveled to Jupiter. He says he did this under the guidance of Harold Puthoff and Russell Targ. (You remember them, don't you?) The journey is especially noteworthy because Swann never left the ground, let alone the building. Instead, he used a convenient stay-at-home method called remote viewing. Remote viewing has become all the rage with psychic investigators since its emergence in the 1970s. Puthoff and Targ are its chief promoters, but the CIA is also very hot on it. (More about that later.)

In a remote-viewing exercise, the subject is given a target, identified only by a set of coordinates. Usually, these are the target site's latitude and longitude. The subject then "travels" to the target via some mysterious psychic means and describes or draws what he or she sees. Researchers compare the subject's description to the actual site, and if it matches, it is scored as a hit.

Normally, in remote-viewing tests, the subject doesn't get to pick the target. (That would be cheating, wouldn't it?) But Puthoff and Targ saw nothing wrong in allowing Swann to

Were Ingo Swann's visions of Jupiter a result of remote viewing? Or were they inspired by photos of the swirling planet?

go to Jupiter. It was the early 1970s, and *Pioneer 10* had not yet reached the planet and begun sending back the first pictures. But astronomers already knew a little something about Jupiter. So Swann had to journey only as far as the public library for his information. But it was to Jupiter he said he went, and this is what he told Targ and Putoff he saw.

Swann confirmed that Jupiter has stripes. This was hardly news. The stripes are clearly visible through a telescope and had been photographed hundreds of times. Jupiter also has a cloud cover, said Swann, a very thick atmosphere, and tremendous winds. He was right, but again, nothing new.

Swann also reported a 30,000-foot-high mountain range, a sandy surface, and an area of liquid with icebergs floating in it. This isn't even close to reality, but icebergs must have seemed logical to Swann. Jupiter is cold, and cold places usually have ice. And since Jupiter is the biggest planet in the solar system, it ought to have a big mountain range, right?

Mentioning the sandy surface took guts, but Swann may have figured that when *Pioneer 10* arrived for the photo session, it wouldn't be able to see enough through all those clouds to disprove his claims.

Swann supposedly said that Jupiter has a ring—which it does. But it wasn't until *Pioneer 10* got close enough to photograph the thin ring that astronomers learned about it. This hit certainly seems to support Swann's claim that he obtained his information about Jupiter through remote viewing. But if that's true, why didn't Swann get everything right? After all, he assured everybody he had been there!

Courtney Brown's psychic journey was even more interesting. Brown, an associate professor of political science, claims to have taken training lessons in remote viewing from a member of the military. In the late 1960s, intelligence sources informed Washington that the Russians were conducting remote-viewing experiments and were very serious about it. The research was running up a tab of 60 million rubles annually.

Not to be outdone, in 1970 the CIA decided to enter the remote-viewing business. They called the initial program SCANATE, but over the years, it has had many names. STAR GATE is probably the most imaginative. People who seemed to have ESP ability were chosen to take part and then trained in remote viewing. (Ingo Swann was a first-round draft pick.)

Courtney Brown did his remote viewing in a featureless, gray office. He sat at a table with a pen and a stack of paper on which he made his drawings. His trainer presented him with two sets of coordinates, and "at this point," says Brown, "my autonomic nervous system [began] to activate my hand." He is suggesting, in other words, that he wasn't consciously controlling his drawing.

Brown begins to narrate. He sees a mountain; a flat, sandy area; a house, and a pyramid. The pyramid is enormous. It is made of stone, "solid but hollow at the same time." Brown enters. He sees several tunnels, follows one, and winds up outside the pyramid. It is windy. The mountain is erupting. People are running every which way. They are panicked. Brown wonders if he is seeing the city of Pompeii when Mount Vesuvius erupted in A.D. 79. (Time travel?) But no, he decides. There weren't any pyramids in Pompeii. The session ends.

Brown asks his trainer where he was sent, and he is given a folder. He opens the folder and finds a NASA photograph. It shows the Cydonia region of Mars. "There," says Brown, "[was] the pyramid, clear as day."

Something quite fascinating may have happened here, but it certainly wasn't remote viewing. The pyramid that Brown claims he "entered" is actually a natural land formation. It is a hill that looks like a pyramid only because of the way it was photographed. But a number of years before, when Richard Hoagland and a few others had seen *Viking 1*'s pictures of the Cydonia region, they all believed they were looking at evidence of a Martian civilization. They imagined pyramids, walled cities, fortresses, and, most famous of all, a giant stone face. The face, they added, might even be a message to earthlings.

Hoagland quickly wrote a book, which was published in 1987. It's full of tantalizing photographs, elaborate measurements, and wild speculation. Like all good imaginative stories, it captured the public's interest. Before long, everyone was talking about "the face on Mars" and the Martian pyramids. This is when Brown came on the scene.

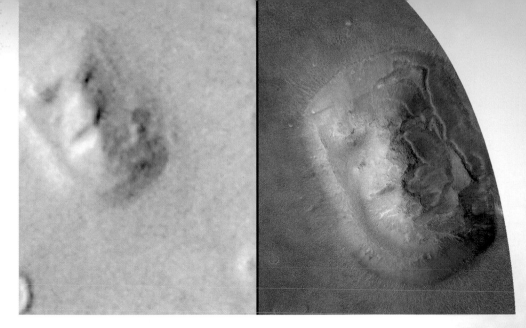

The "face on Mars" *(left)*, as seen in an early image taken in the 1970s looks much different in the high-resolution image *(right)* taken in 2001.

In 1998 the *Mars Global Surveyor* returned another batch of pictures of the Cydonia region. But this time, the sun was at a different angle and the shadows were shorter. And the pyramids? Well, they had all vanished into the thin Martian air. So what did Courtney Brown "visit" during his remote-viewing session? It is likely that Professor Brown visited Hoagland's book and his own imagination.

"Yes, but what about the photograph?" you may be thinking. "He still got the target right." But did he really? Brown didn't describe the Cydonia region. He described an *imagined scene inspired by Hoagland's book.*

"Well, yes," you say, "but he couldn't have known before the session began that Mars was the target. He must have at least used ESP to determine what the target was, then relied on Hoagland's book to fill in the details."

Aha! But perhaps he did know before the session began. Brown's session was not conducted under controlled conditions. He simply sat down with his "trainer," and off they went. Furthermore, the trainer chose the target, and it was one he had used before. When Brown was shown the target picture, he said, "You're kidding. You sent me . . . to Mars?" And his trainer replied, "Hey, I like sending my students there." Could Brown have learned the target ahead of time from another student? It's certainly possible. And there's one more thing to consider. The only word we have that any of this happened is Brown's.

Recently, the government declassified one of its top-secret remote-viewing sessions. In 1975 a subject was asked to describe a Soviet military complex known as URDF-3. The subject was given the coordinates 50°9'59" N and 78°22'22" E. He was then shown the target location on a map. He was told the target was a scientific test area located 25 to 30 miles southwest of the Irtysh River.

The session began. The first thing the subject reported seeing was a complex of low buildings. When asked to describe the general area, he said the road leading from the river passes through a gorge. (It doesn't.)

He saw an outdoor pool, measuring 60 feet by 150 feet. (No pool exists at the complex.)

He saw a line of telephone poles 400 yards southeast of the complex. (There are no such telephone poles.)

When asked if he saw a railroad anywhere near the complex, he said the closest one was 60 miles away. (There is actually a railway *within* the complex.)

He described a small village, an airstrip, and a cluster of pine trees but did not correctly locate any of them.

Building One, he said, was dominant. It was 80 feet by 160 feet and centrally positioned. All the other buildings seemed to "pivot off of it." (There is no building at the complex that matches this description.)

And so it went. It is hard to know if the government was satisfied with the subject's performance. Would you be?

So what exactly is remote viewing? Well, nobody really knows. The government obviously thinks it might be *something*, and if they have genuine remote viewers on the payroll, it's their little secret. But not everyone is convinced that remote viewing can really be done. In fact, ESP in general is far from proven. It is the sense that may, indeed, be nonsense—hyped, faked, and experimentally fudged. But it may also be the gift that came without an instruction book. Something here is truly unexplained. We just don't know what.

Books// Krull, Kathleen. *They Saw the Future: Oracles, Psychics, Scientists, Great Thinkers and Pretty Good Guessers.* New York: Atheneum Books for Young Readers, 1999.
This illustrated biography tells the stories of 12 individuals or groups who attempted to imagine the future. The author's humorous, skeptical tone reveals how some seers proved more accurate than others.

Oxlade, Chris. *The Mystery of ESP.* Chicago: Heinemann Library, 2002.
This book explores the scientific investigation of ESP through photographs and personal accounts.

Videos// *History Undercover: Psychic Espionage.* 2002. New York: A&E Home Video.
This documentary describes the CIA's efforts to develop agents with ESP in response to similar efforts in the Soviet Union during the 1970s.

Matilda. 1996. Culver City, CA: TriStar Pictures.
Psychokinetic powers help an unusually intelligent girl take revenge on her bumbling parents and a cruel school principal. Based on the children's book by Roald Dahl.

Websites// The Skeptiseum
<http://www.skeptiseum.org/exhibits/psychic%20phenomena/index.html>
This online "Skeptical Museum of the Paranormal" features an exhibit on astrology, Zener cards, and various types of fortune-telling.

Zener Card ESP Test
<http://moebius.psy.ed.ac.uk/~paul/zener.html>
At this site, you can take a Zener card test to experience how scientists test subjects for ESP. The test results explain how many "hits" the test taker made and how that score compares to chance.

>> About the Author

Born in Baltimore, Maryland, Judith Herbst grew up in Queens, New York, where she learned to jump double Dutch with amazing skill. She has since lost that ability. A former English teacher, she ran away from school in her tenure year to become a writer. Her first book for kids was *Sky Above and Words Beyond,* whose title, she admits, was much too long. She loves to write and would rather be published, she says, than be rich, which has turned out to be the case. Herbst spends summers in Maine on a lake with her cats and laptop.

>> Photo Acknowledgments

Photographs and illustrations in this book are used with the permission of: Fortean Picture Library, pp. 6, 10, 12, 21, 26 (Guy Lyon Playfair), 28, 29 (Dr. Elmar R. Gruber), 33; © SuperStock, p. 8; © Bettmann/CORBIS, pp. 11, 19, 32; Library of Congress, p. 22 (LC-USZ62-19851); © CORBIS, p. 23; ParaPictures Archive, Munich, p. 34; Courtesy of NASA and the Lunar and Planetary Institute, p. 40; AFP/CORBIS, p. 43. Illustrations by Bill Hauser, pp. 4–5, 18, 20, 24, 30, 35, 38.

Front cover illustration by Bill Hauser.